"It's hard to connect with your child without first understanding where they are. As counselors and speakers at parenting events across the country, we spend a great deal of time teaching parents about development. To know *where* your child is—not just physically, but emotionally, socially, and spiritually, helps you to truly know and understand *who* your child is. And that understanding is the key to connecting. The Phase Guides give you the tools to do just that. Our wise friends Reggie and Kristen have put together an insightful, hopeful, practical, and literal year-by-year guide that will help you to understand and connect with your child at every age."

SISSY GOFF
M.ED., LPC-MHSP, DIRECTOR OF CHILD & ADOLESCENT COUNSELING AT DAYSTAR COUNSELING MINISTRIES IN NASHVILLE, TENNESSEE, SPEAKER AND AUTHOR OF ARE MY KIDS ON TRACK?

"These resources for parents are fantastically empowering, absolute in their simplicity, and completely doable in every way. The hard work that has gone into the Phase Project will echo through the ne powerful ways."

JENNIFER WALKER
RN BSN, AUTHOR AND FOUNDER OF MOMS ON

D1637306

"We all know where we want to end up in our ｐ can seem like an unsolved mystery. Through the Phase Project series, Reggie Joiner and Kristen Ivy team up to help us out. The result is a resource that guides us through the different seasons of raising children, and provides a road map to parenting in such a way that we finish up with very few regrets."

SANDRA STANLEY
FOSTER CARE ADVOCATE, BLOGGER, WIFE TO ANDY STANLEY, MOTHER OF THREE

"Not only are the Phase Guides the most creative and well-thought-out guides to parenting I have ever encountered, these books are ESSENTIAL to my daily parenting. With a 13-year-old, 11-year-old, and 9-year-old at home, I am swimming in their wake of daily drama and delicacy. These books are a reminder to enjoy every second. Because it's just a phase."

CARLOS WHITTAKER
AUTHOR, SPEAKER, FATHER OF THREE

"As the founder of Minnie's Food Pantry, I see thousands of people each month with children who will benefit from the advice, guidance, and nuggets of information on how to celebrate and understand the phases of their child's life. Too often we feel like we're losing our mind when sweet little Johnny starts to change his behavior into a person we do not know. I can't wait to start implementing the principles of these books with my clients to remind them . . . it's just a phase."

CHERYL JACKSON
FOUNDER OF MINNIE'S FOOD PANTRY, AWARD-WINNING PHILANTHROPIST, AND GRANDMOTHER

"I began exploring this resource with my counselor hat on, thinking how valuable this will be for the many parents I spend time with in my office. I ended up taking my counselor hat off and putting on my parent hat. Then I kept thinking about friends who are teachers, coaches, youth pastors, and children's ministers, who would want this in their hands. What a valuable resource the Orange team has given us to better understand and care for the kids and adolescents we love. I look forward to sharing it broadly."

DAVID THOMAS
LMSW, DIRECTOR OF FAMILY COUNSELING, DAYSTAR COUNSELING MINISTRIES, SPEAKER AND AUTHOR OF ARE MY KIDS ON TRACK? *AND* WILD THINGS: THE ART OF NURTURING BOYS

"I have always wished someone would hand me a manual for parenting. Well, the Phase Guides are more than what I wished for. They guide, inspire, and challenge me as a parent—while giving me incredible insight into my children at each age and phase. Our family will be using these every year!"

COURTNEY DEFEO
AUTHOR OF IN THIS HOUSE, WE WILL GIGGLE, *MOTHER OF TWO*

"As I speak to high school students and their parents, I always wonder to myself: What would it have been like if they had better seen what was coming next? What if they had a guide that would tell them what to expect and how to be ready? What if they could anticipate what is predictable about the high school years before they actually hit? These Phase Guides give a parent that kind of preparation so they can have a plan when they need it most."

JOSH SHIPP
AUTHOR, TEEN EXPERT, AND YOUTH SPEAKER

"The Phase Guides are incredibly creative, well researched, and filled with inspirational actions for everyday life. Each age-specific guide is catalytic for equipping parents to lead and love their kids as they grow up. I'm blown away and deeply encouraged by the content and by its creators. I highly recommend Phase resources for all parents, teachers, and influencers of children. This is the stuff that challenges us and changes our world. Get them. Read them. And use them!"

DANIELLE STRICKLAND
OFFICER WITH THE SALVATION ARMY, AUTHOR, SPEAKER, MOTHER OF TWO

"It's true that parenting is one of life's greatest joys but it is not without its challenges. If we're honest, parenting can sometimes feel like trying to choreograph a dance to an ever-changing beat. It can be clumsy and riddled with well-meaning missteps. If parenting is a dance, this Parenting Guide is a skilled instructor refining your technique and helping you move gracefully to a steady beat. For those of us who love to plan ahead, this guide will help you anticipate what's to come so you can be poised and ready to embrace the moments you want to enjoy."

TINA NAIDOO
MSSW, LCSW EXECUTIVE DIRECTOR, THE POTTER'S HOUSE OF DALLAS, INC.

PARENTING YOUR SECOND GRADER

A GUIDE TO MAKING THE MOST OF THE "SOUNDS LIKE FUN!" PHASE

KRISTEN IVY AND REGGIE JOINER

PARENTING YOUR SECOND GRADER
A GUIDE TO MAKING THE MOST OF THE
"SOUNDS LIKE FUN!" PHASE

Published by Orange, a division of The reThink Group, Inc.,
5870 Charlotte Lane, Suite 300,
Cumming, GA 30040 U.S.A.

©2017 Kristen Ivy and Reggie Joiner
Authors: Kristen Ivy and Reggie Joiner
Lead Editor: Karen Wilson
Editing Team: Melanie Williams, Hannah Crosby, Sherry Surratt

Art Direction: Ryan Boon and Hannah Crosby
Book Design: FiveStone and Sharon van Rossum

Printed in the United States of America
First Edition 2017
1 2 3 4 5 6 7 8 9 10

Special thanks to:

*Jim Burns, Ph.D for guidance and consultation
on having conversations about sexual integrity*

*Jon Acuff for guidance and consultation on having
conversations about technological responsibility*

*Jean Sumner, MD for guidance and consultation
on having conversations about healthy habits*

*Every educator, counselor, community leader, and
researcher who invested in the Phase Project*

TABLE OF CONTENTS

HOW TO USE THIS ~~BOOK~~ ~~JOURNAL~~ GUIDE

The guide you hold in your hand doesn't have very many words, but it does have a lot of ideas. Some of these ideas come from thousands of hours of research. Others come from parents, educators, and volunteers who spend every day with kids the same age as yours. This guide won't tell you everything about your kid, but it will tell you a few things about kids at this age.

The best way to use this guide is to take what these pages tell you about second grader and combine it with what you know is true about *your* second grader.

Let's sum it up:

THINGS ABOUT SECOND GRADERS +
THOUGHTS ABOUT *YOUR* SECOND GRADER =
YOUR GUIDE TO THE NEXT 52 WEEKS OF PARENTING

After each idea in this guide, there are pages with a few questions designed to prompt you to think about your kid, your family, and yourself as a parent. The only guarantee we give to parents who use this guide is this: You will mess up some things as a parent this year. Actually, that's a guarantee to every parent, regardless. But you, you picked up this book! You want to be a better parent. And that's what we hope this guide will do: help you parent your kid just a little better, simply because you paused to consider a few ideas that can help you make the most of this phase.

THE SECOND GRADE PHASE

Welcome to the wonderful year of second grade! You're in the phase that is the very essence of childhood.

I've been working with children for over forty years now, and I've been a parent for more than thirty. In my experience, this is the age that brings a smile to my heart more than any other. This up-for-anything, sounds-like-fun bunch is always ready to go.

Want to go camping? "Sounds like fun!"
Want to dance? "Sounds like fun!"
Want to help wash the car with Daddy? "Sounds like fun!"
Want to go to a rodeo? "Sounds like fun!"
Want to make a building out of sugar cubes? "Sounds like fun!"
Want to take guitar lessons? "Sounds like fun!"

Now's the time to rekindle your adventurous side and experience things with your child you've always wanted to try yourself.

Looking back on this phase with my daughters, I remember the temptation my wife and I had to disengage. Our kids were finally reaching a comfortable level of independence. They could ride their bikes to a friend's house. They could make their own snacks in the kitchen. They could read and play on their own with very little help from us.

Let's face it—we wanted to raise independent young women, and we were happy to celebrate their first steps in that direction by enjoying adult conversation for the first time in almost a decade.

While the increased freedom is definitely part of what makes this a sweet season of parenting, don't disengage too much. While you catch your breath, remember there's a lot happening in their second-grade world. And you don't want to miss it. For example, one of the things that I admire about second graders is their understanding of right and wrong. They're eager to know what's right, and they still believe that what you say is true. That means there's a great opportunity for you to instill values that are important to your family and to your child's future.

And here's the great news—all the fun and adventure and memory-making that will make this year fantastic goes hand-in-hand with some of the most important truths you want your kid to learn in this phase. As you play games together, talk about winning and losing. As you wash the car together, talk about the value of hard work and how good it feels to see what you've done. Look for ways to shape their character as you go about doing the many things that "sound like fun."

The sunny second-grade phase won't last forever. Savor and enjoy every crazy adventure it brings. And, don't forget. You're building your child's history. You're making memories together that you both can draw from in the years ahead. Let this phase be the one you tell family stories about for decades to come.

- JIM WIDEMAN
CHILDREN MINISTRY PIONEER, PASTOR, & AUTHOR

52 WEEKS
—
TO PARENT YOUR SECOND GRADER

WHEN YOU SEE
HOW MUCH

Time

YOU HAVE LEFT

—

YOU TEND TO DO

More

WITH THE TIME
YOU HAVE NOW.

THERE ARE APPROXIMATELY

936 WEEKS

FROM THE TIME A BABY IS BORN UNTIL THEY GROW UP AND MOVE TO WHATEVER IS NEXT.

It may seem hard to believe, but on the day your child starts second grade, you only have 572 weeks remaining. And while things like cell phone contracts and learner's permits still feel far away, you're starting to realize your kid is growing up faster than you ever dreamed.

That's why every week counts. Of course, each week might not feel significant. There may be weeks this year when all you feel like you accomplished was checking to make sure they did their homework (most nights). That's okay.

Take a deep breath.
You don't have to get everything done this week.

But what happens in your child's life week after week, year after year, adds up over time. So, it might be a good idea to put a number to your weeks.

MEASURE IT OUT.

Write down the number of weeks that have already passed since your kid was born. Then write down the number of weeks you have left before they graduate high school.

🔑 **HINT:** If you want a little help counting it out, you can download the free Parent Cue app on all mobile platforms.

_____

_____

_____

CREATE A VISUAL COUNTDOWN.

 Find a jar and fill it with one marble for each week you have remaining with your child. Then make a habit of removing one marble every week as a reminder to make the most of your time. Where can you place your visual countdown so you will see it frequently?

_____

_____

_____

_____

_____

Which day of the week is best for you to remove a marble?

_____

_____

_____

Is there anything you want to do each week as you remove a marble? (Examples: say a prayer, play a game, retell one favorite memory from this past week)

_____

_____

_____

_____

_____

_____

_____

_____

_____

_____

_____

_____

EVERY PHASE IS A
TIMEFRAME
IN A KID'S LIFE
WHEN YOU CAN
LEVERAGE
DISTINCTIVE
OPPORTUNITIES
TO INFLUENCE
THEIR

future.

YOU ONLY HAVE
52 WEEKS
WITH YOUR SECOND GRADER

while they are still in second grade.

Then they will be in third grade,

and you will never know them as a second grader again.

Or, to say it another way:

Before you know it, your kid will grow up a little more and . . .

try out for a sports team.

ask to go to a slumber party.

have a homework question you don't understand.

The point is this: The phase you are in now has remarkable potential. And before the end of second grade, there are some distinctive opportunities you don't want to miss. So, as you count down the next 52 weeks, pay attention to what makes these weeks uniquely different from the time you've already spent together and the weeks you will have when they move on to the next phase.

What are some things you have noticed about your second grader in this phase that you really enjoy?

_____

_____

_____

_____

_____

_____

_____

_____

_____

_____

_____

_____

_____

_____

_____

_____

_____

_____

_____

What is something new you are learning as a parent during this phase?

_____

_____

_____

_____

_____

_____

_____

_____

_____

_____

_____

_____

_____

_____

_____

_____

_____

_____

_____

SECOND GRADE

—

THE PHASE WHEN FAIRNESS MATTERS MOST, DIFFERENCES GET NOTICED, AND YOUR ENTHUSIASTIC KID THINKS ANYTHING,

"Sounds like fun!"

FAIRNESS MATTERS.

Cops. CSI. Nancy Drew. Barney Fife. Whatever the badge, your child will quickly apprehend and convict you for offenses of unfairness. They may also report the offenses of others, including teachers, classmates, or puppies—if they detect a preference that isn't in their favor.

DIFFERENCES DISPLAY THEIR UNIQUENESS.

Your second grader's brain is changing in some incredible ways, and they are beginning to notice, "Not everyone is like me." Until now, everyone was pretty equal. Seriously, what kindergartner isn't "the best" at everything? By second grade, kids take notice of qualities that make one kid "athletic" and another "artistic."

THIS PHASE IS A BLEND OF CAPABLE AND DEPENDENT.

You are entering the golden years of childhood. No one should have a favorite phase, but if you like this phase a whole lot, you aren't alone. Your kid is impressionable, eager, and excited about what you are excited about. If you think something sounds like fun, it won't take much to convince them it really is fun.

THIS

YEAR

YOUR

SECOND

GRADER

IS

changing.

PHYSICALLY

- Continues losing baby teeth (incisors and canines)
- Grows approximately three inches and gains seven pounds, typically in spurts
- Improving hand-eye coordination
- Needs 10-11 hours of sleep each night

SOCIALLY

- May struggle in highly competitive situations
- Often prefers independent work and alone time
- Places a high value on fairness and consistency
- Shows gender preference for friends

MENTALLY

- Concentrates on one activity up to 30 minutes
- Logically interprets cause and effect
- Has a better understanding of time (seconds, minutes, hours, days. . .)
- Learns well through hands-on activities, problem solving, codes, and puzzles
- Beginning to notice that people have different perspectives than their own

EMOTIONALLY

- Better able to control their emotions
- Tends to be perfectionistic (easily embarrassed by failure)
- May confuse "I feel . . . " with "I am . . . "
- Thrives with routines and clear boundaries
- Highly sensitive to harsh criticism, tone, and body language

What are some changes you are noticing in your second grader?

_____

_____

_____

_____

_____

_____

You may disagree with some of the characteristics we've shared about second graders. That's because every second grader is unique. What makes your second grader different from second graders in general?

_____

_____

_____

_____

_____

_____

_____

What do you want to remember about this year with your second grader?

Mark this page. Throughout the year, write down a few simple things you want to remember. If you want to be really thorough, there are about 52 blank lines. But some weeks, you may spend so much time trying to get them to finish brushing their teeth *(seriously, what's taking them so long?)* that you forget to write down a memory. That's okay.

_____

_____

_____

_____

_____

_____

_____

_____

_____

_____

_____

_____

_____

_____

_____

_____

_____

_____

_____

_____

SIX THINGS

—

EVERY KID
NEEDS

YOUR KID **NEEDS 6 THINGS OVER TIME**

LOVE

STORIES

WORDS

WORK

PEOPLE

FUN

OVER THE NEXT 572 WEEKS YOUR CHILD WILL NEED MANY THINGS.

Some of the things your kid needs will change from phase to phase, but there are six things every kid needs at every phase. In fact, these things may be the most important things you give your kid.

EVERY KID, AT EVERY PHASE, NEEDS . . .

♡ LOVE

to give them a
sense of WORTH.

📖 STORIES —

to give them a bigger
PERSPECTIVE.

🏋 WORK

to give them
PURPOSE.

♟ FUN

to give them
CONNECTION.

👥 PEOPLE

to give them
BELONGING.

💬 WORDS

to give them
DIRECTION.

The next few pages are designed to help you think about how you will give your child these six things, right now—while they are in second grade.

EVERY KID

NEEDS

love

OVER TIME

—

TO GIVE THEM

A SENSE OF

worth.

♡ ONE QUESTION YOUR SECOND GRADER IS ASKING

Your second grader is becoming increasingly self-aware—aware of their thoughts, aware of their abilities, and very aware of their mistakes. Even though your kid is gaining independence in some wonderful ways, don't miss the internal struggle of this phase.

Your second grader is asking one major question:

"DO I HAVE WHAT IT TAKES?"

They want to know they have what it takes to make the team, to get the grade, and to measure up to their own (and your) standards. You give your kid the love they need when you do one thing:

ENGAGE their interests.

Second graders are interested in learning new skills. So, engage your second grader's interests by . . .

showing curiosity about their activities,

encouraging their efforts, and

helping them push through set-backs.

You are probably doing more than you realize to show your second grader just how much you love them. Make a list of the ways you already show up consistently to engage your child's interests.

🏆 You may need to look at this list on a bad day to remember what a great parent you are.

_____

_____

_____

_____

_____

_____

_____

_____

_____

_____

_____

_____

_____

_____

_____

Engaging your child's interests requires paying attention to what they like. What does your second grader seem to enjoy the most right now?

_____

_____

_____

_____

_____

_____

_____

_____

_____

_____

_____

_____

_____

_____

_____

_____

_____

_____

It's impossible to love anyone with the persistence a second grader requires unless you have a little time for yourself. What can you do to refuel each week so you are able to give your second grader the love they need?

_____

_____

_____

_____

_____

_____

_____

_____

_____

_____

_____

_____

_____

_____

_____

Who do you have around you supporting you this year?

_____

_____

_____

_____

_____

_____

_____

_____

_____

_____

_____

_____

_____

_____

_____

_____

_____

_____

_____

_____

_____

EVERY KID

NEEDS

stories

OVER TIME

—

TO GIVE THEM

A BIGGER

perspective.

BOOKS TO READ
WITH YOUR SECOND GRADER

BEFOREVER (SERIES)
by American Girl

CAM JANSEN AND THE MYSTERY OF THE BABE RUTH BASEBALL
by David A. Adler

FLY GUY (SERIES)
by Tedd Arnold

IVY + BEAN (SERIES)
by Annie Barrows

FRECKLE JUICE
FUDGE-A-MANIA
by Judy Blume

THE FAMILY UNDER THE BRIDGE
by Natalie Savage Carlson

HENRY HUGGINS (SERIES)
by Beverly Cleary

THE MOUSE AND THE MOTORCYCLE
by Beverly Cleary

MERCY WATSON (SERIES)
by Kate DiCamillo

THE TALE OF DESPEREAUX
by Kate DiCamillo

THE HUNDRED DRESSES
by Eleanor Estes

IN THE TREE HOUSE
by Andrew Larsen

JUDY MOODY (SERIES)
by Megan McDonald

THE COMPLETE TALES OF WINNIE-THE-POOH
by A. A. Milne

AMELIA BEDELIA (SERIES)
by Peggy Parish

THE RANDOM HOUSE BOOK OF POETRY FOR CHILDREN
by Jack Prelutsky

TALES FOR VERY PICKY EATERS
by Josh Schneider

THE BOXCAR CHILDREN (SERIES)
by Gertrude Chandler Warner

THE LITTLE HOUSE (SERIES)
by Laura Ingles Wilder

COMING ON HOME SOON
by Jacqueline Woodson

Tell your second grader's story. Do you have a photo album, a website, or a baby book? What are some ways you can preserve and retell the story of your kid's first years?

_____

_____

_____

_____

_____

_____

_____

_____

_____

_____

_____

_____

_____

_____

_____

_____

_____

Tell your story. *(Okay, maybe not all of it, right now.)* What are some life stories you can share with your second grader?

_____

_____

_____

_____

_____

_____

_____

_____

_____

_____

_____

_____

_____

_____

_____

_____

_____

_____

_____

Tell your family story. What do you want to record now so you can share it with your second grader later? Consider starting a family journal, a video archive, a travel scrapbook, or a drawer of things connected to special memories. Write down some ideas that might fit your family's values and style.

_____

_____

_____

_____

_____

_____

_____

_____

_____

_____

_____

_____

_____

_____

EVERY KID

NEEDS

work

OVER TIME

—

TO GIVE

THEM

purpose.

WORK YOUR
SECOND GRADER CAN DO

TIE SHOES

BATHE AND BRUSH TEETH INDEPENDENTLY

DO HOMEWORK
(with assistance)

PACK FOR A TRIP
(if you make the packing list)

ADDRESS, STAMP, AND MAIL A LETTER

HANDWASH THE DISHES

FOLD AND PUT AWAY LAUNDRY

USE A CAN OPENER, CHEESE GRATER, TOASTER OVEN, MICROWAVE, OR ELECTRIC MIXER

COUNT MONEY AND MAKE CHANGE

MAKE THEIR BED AND CLEAN THEIR ROOM
(even if it doesn't always stay that way)

USE A SCREWDRIVER OR WRENCH

WRAP A PRESENT
(depending on how much you care about the result)

What are some jobs you can give to your second grader?

_____

_____

_____

_____

_____

_____

_____

_____

_____

_____

_____

_____

_____

_____

_____

_____

_____

_____

_____

Some days it's easier than others to motivate your second grader to do their work. What are some strategies that tend to keep your second grader motivated?

🔒 HINT: Maybe try a few things like, "When we finish, we will go out—just you and me."

_____

_____

_____

_____

_____

_____

_____

_____

_____

_____

_____

_____

_____

_____

_____

What are things you hope your second grader will be able to do independently in the next phase?

_____

_____

_____

_____

_____

_____

_____

_____

_____

_____

_____

_____

_____

_____

_____

_____

_____

How are you helping them develop those skills now?

_____

_____

_____

_____

_____

_____

_____

_____

_____

_____

_____

_____

_____

_____

_____

_____

_____

_____

_____

_____

_____

EVERY KID

NEEDS

fun

OVER TIME

—

TO GIVE

THEM

connection.

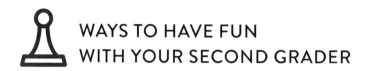

WAYS TO HAVE FUN WITH YOUR SECOND GRADER

GAMES:

CLUE JR. ®	**BLOKUS®**	**BINGO**
HEDBANZ®	**QUIRKLE®**	**CONNECT FOUR®**
MONOPOLY®	**CHECKERS**	**SPOT IT®**
GUESS WHO?®	**CHESS**	**TOPPLE®**
BATTLESHIP®	**DOMINOS**	**SQUARE UP®**

ACTIVITIES:

CRAFTS WITH BEADS OR STRING	**CUP-SONG AROUND THE TABLE**	**KARAOKE**
ART OF ANY KIND (colored pencils, markers, paint, stencils)	**CHARADES**	**PAPER FOOTBALL**
	HANGMAN	**PAPER AIRPLANES**
	DOTS	**WATER BALLOONS**
SPOONS (card game)		**LEGOS®**
	KEEP AWAY	
PHASE 10®, SKIP-BO® (card games)	**FREEZE TAG**	**BEANBAG TOSS**
	MAD LIBS®	**50-100 PIECE JIGSAW PUZZLES**
FOUR SQUARE		

What are some games and activities you and your second grader enjoy?

_____

_____

_____

_____

_____

_____

_____

_____

_____

_____

_____

_____

_____

_____

_____

_____

_____

_____

_____

When are the best times of the day, or week, to set aside for you to just have fun with your second grader?

_____

_____

_____

_____

_____

_____

_____

_____

_____

_____

_____

_____

_____

_____

_____

_____

_____

_____

_____

_____

_____

Some days are *extra* fun days. What are some ways you want to celebrate the special days coming up this year?

CHILD'S BIRTHDAY

_____

_____

_____

_____

_____

_____

_____

_____

_____

_____

_____

_____

_____

_____

_____

_____

HOLIDAYS

EVERY KID

NEEDS

people

OVER TIME

—

TO GIVE

THEM

belonging.

ADULTS WHO MIGHT INFLUENCE YOUR SECOND GRADER

PARENTS

NEIGHBORS

CHURCH LEADERS

GRANDPARENTS

PARENT'S FRIENDS

COACHES

AUNTS & UNCLES

SECOND GRADE TEACHER

BABYSITTERS

List at least five adults who have influence in your second grader's life right now.

🔑 HINT: If you aren't sure, you can ask them.

_____

_____

_____

_____

_____

_____

_____

_____

_____

_____

_____

_____

_____

_____

_____

_____

What is one one way these adults could help you and your second grader this year?

_____

_____

_____

_____

_____

_____

_____

_____

_____

_____

_____

_____

_____

_____

_____

_____

_____

_____

_____

_____

What are a few ways you could show these adults appreciation for the significant role they play in your child's life?

_____

_____

_____

_____

_____

_____

_____

_____

_____

_____

_____

_____

_____

_____

_____

_____

_____

_____

EVERY KID

NEEDS

words

OVER TIME

—

TO GIVE

THEM

direction.

WORDS YOUR SECOND GRADER NEEDS TO HEAR

GOOD MORNING!

I HAVE NOTICED . . .

I HOPE YOU KNOW . . .

I LOVE YOU

HAVE FUN

KEEP TRYING

I'M REALLY PROUD WHEN . . .

PLEASE

THANK YOU

WORK HARD

I'VE BEEN THINKING . . .

GOOD NIGHT!

I'M SORRY

BE KIND

I ENJOY SPENDING TIME WITH YOU

If words over time give a kid direction, what word (or words) describes your hopes for your second grader in this phase?

DETERMINED	MOTIVATED	GENTLE
ENCOURAGING	INTROSPECTIVE	PASSIONATE
SELF-ASSURED	ENTHUSIASTIC	PATIENT
ASSERTIVE	JOYFUL	FORGIVING
DARING	ENTERTAINING	CREATIVE
INSIGHTFUL	INDEPENDENT	WITTY
COMPASSIONATE	OBSERVANT	AMBITIOUS
AMIABLE	SENSITIVE	HELPFUL
EASY-GOING	ENDEARING	AUTHENTIC
DILIGENT	ADVENTUROUS	INVENTIVE
PROACTIVE	HONEST	DEVOTED
OPTIMISTIC	CURIOUS	GENUINE
FEARLESS	DEPENDABLE	ATTENTIVE
AFFECTIONATE	GENEROUS	HARMONIOUS
COURAGEOUS	COMMITTED	EMPATHETIC
CAUTIOUS	RESPONSIBLE	COURAGEOUS
DEVOTED	TRUSTWORTHY	FLEXIBLE
INQUISITIVE	THOUGHTFUL	CAREFUL
PATIENT	LOYAL	NURTURING
OPEN-MINDED	KIND	RELIABLE

Where can you place those words in your home so they will remind you what you want for your child this year?

_____

_____

_____

_____

_____

_____

_____

_____

_____

_____

_____

_____

_____

_____

_____

_____

_____

_____

_____

_____

The words we use determine the way we think. Are there words you have chosen to not say *(or not to say often)*? What do you want for your kid to know about these words, and how do you want them to respond if they hear them?

_____

_____

_____

_____

_____

_____

_____

_____

_____

_____

_____

_____

_____

_____

_____

_____

FOUR CONVERSATIONS

—

TO HAVE IN THIS PHASE

WHEN YOU KNOW
WHERE YOU WANT
TO GO,

AND YOU KNOW
WHERE YOU ARE
NOW,

YOU CAN ALWAYS
DO SOMETHING

TO MOVE IN A
BETTER DIRECTION.

OVER THE NEXT 572 WEEKS OF YOUR CHILD'S LIFE, SOME CONVERSATIONS MAY MATTER MORE THAN OTHERS.

WHAT YOU SAY, FOR EXAMPLE, REGARDING . . .

Star Wars

Shark attacks

and Justin Timberlake

MIGHT HAVE LESS IMPACT ON THEIR FUTURE THAN WHAT YOU SAY REGARDING . . .

Health

Sex

Technology

or Faith.

The next pages are about the conversations that matter most. On the left page is a destination—what you might want to be true in your kid's life 572 weeks from now. On the right page is a goal for conversations with your second grader and a few suggestions about what you might want to say.

Healthy habits

—

LEARNING TO STRENGTHEN MY BODY THROUGH EXERCISE, NUTRITION, AND SELF-ADVOCACY

THIS YEAR YOU WILL

DEVELOP POSITIVE ROUTINES

SO YOUR CHILD WILL ENJOY EATING WELL
AND EXERCISING OFTEN.

Maintain a good relationship with your pediatrician, and schedule
a well visit at least once per year. You can also begin to develop
healthy habits for your second grader with a few simple words.

SAY THINGS LIKE . . .

CAN YOU CUT OUT THE BISCUITS?
(Teach cooking basics.)

PEOPLE HAVE DIFFERENT BODY TYPES LIKE THEY HAVE DIFFERENT EYE COLORS.
(Use positive words to talk about different body types.)

THAT'S A BIG SERVING. WE CAN TAKE THAT HOME IF YOU DON'T FINISH.
(Talk about serving sizes.)

I LOVE TO WATCH YOU PLAY!

THE MAYONNAISE CAN'T SIT IN THE SUN ALL DAY.
(Teach food safety.)

LET'S PLAY FREEZE TAG.

What are some activities you can do with your second grader that require a little bit of exercise? *(They may not call it exercise, but if you get a little winded that counts.)*

_____

_____

_____

_____

_____

_____

_____

_____

_____

_____

_____

_____

_____

_____

_____

_____

_____

_____

Kids who cook learn about what ingredients are in the things they eat. What are some simple ways your second grader can help you in the kitchen?

_____

_____

_____

_____

_____

_____

_____

_____

_____

_____

_____

_____

_____

_____

_____

_____

_____

Who will help you monitor and improve your second grader's health?

_____

_____

_____

_____

_____

_____

_____

_____

_____

_____

_____

_____

_____

_____

_____

What are your own health goals for this year? How can you improve the habits in your own life—*You know, even if most of your athletic time is spent sitting in the stands cheering?*

_____

_____

_____

_____

_____

_____

_____

_____

_____

_____

_____

_____

_____

_____

_____

_____

_____

_____

Sexual integrity

—

GUARDING MY
POTENTIAL FOR
INTIMACY THROUGH
APPROPRIATE
BOUNDARIES
AND MUTUAL
RESPECT

THIS YEAR YOU WILL

INFORM THEM ABOUT HOW THINGS WORK

SO YOUR CHILD WILL UNDERSTAND BIOLOGY
AND BUILD SOCIAL SKILLS.

This is a good year to be intentional about having more thorough talks with your child about marriage, conception, and body changes that will happen with puberty. These topics are likely to come up at school, and it's best if your kid knows you are available to talk about them.

SAY THINGS LIKE . . .

"CAN WE TALK MORE ABOUT THIS ANOTHER TIME?"
(Always finish the conversation with room to pick it back up again later.)

"GOD MADE SEX AND DESIGNED IT TO BE A GOOD GIFT FOR A HUSBAND AND WIFE."

"SEX IS PRIVATE, IT'S NOT SOMETHING WE WATCH OR LOOK AT."

"WHAT HAVE YOU HEARD ABOUT SEX?"

IT'S NATURAL TO BE CURIOUS ABOUT OUR BODIES.

I'M SO GLAD YOU ASKED ME.

"WHEN A GIRL STARTS TO BECOME A WOMAN, SHE WILL . . ."

"WHEN A BOY STARTS TO BECOME A MAN, HE WILL . . ."

When it comes to your child's sexuality, what do you hope is true for them 572 weeks from now?

_____

_____

_____

_____

_____

_____

_____

_____

_____

_____

_____

_____

_____

_____

_____

_____

_____

_____

Write down a few things you want to communicate to your second grader about body changes, about sex, and about marriage. *(You don't have to tell them everything now, or in one talk. This should be many talks—over time.)*

For a little help, check out resources like *How God Makes Babies* by Dr. Jim Burns, *Simple Truths* by Mary Flo Ridley, or *Before I Was Born* by Stan and Brenna Jones.

_____

_____

_____

_____

_____

_____

_____

_____

_____

_____

_____

_____

_____

_____

_____

_____

Follow up. Anytime you talk to your second grader about sex, you may walk away feeling like there were things you didn't say that you wish you would have said, or things you said that you wish you had said better. Use this space to reflect. What do you want to communicate better next time?

_____

_____

_____

_____

_____

_____

_____

_____

_____

_____

_____

_____

_____

_____

_____

_____

_____

_____

_____

_____

_____

_____

_____

_____

_____

_____

Technological responsibility

—

LEVERAGING THE
POTENTIAL OF ONLINE
EXPERIENCES TO
ENHANCE MY OFFLINE
COMMUNITY
AND SUCCESS

THIS YEAR YOU WILL

EXPLORE THE POSSIBILITIES

SO YOUR CHILD WILL UNDERSTAND CORE VALUES AND BUILD ONLINE SKILLS.

Your second grader is smarter than you when it comes to devices—it's okay. That's normal. But, even though your kid is a digital native, they still need an adult guide as they continue to explore all the great things they can do with technology.

SAY THINGS LIKE . . .

LET ME SEE WHAT YOU DID.
(Show interest in what they do with technology.)

"NEVER POST A PHONE NUMBER OR ADDRESS WITHOUT CHECKING WITH ME."
(Kids are often naïve about sharing personal content with strangers.)

CAN WE PLAY TOGETHER?
(Make technology social.)

"I DON'T KNOW, BUT WE CAN LOOK THAT UP TOGETHER."
(Use technology to enhance your conversations.)

"YOU HAVE ____ MINUTES OF SCREEN TIME FOR TODAY."
(Set limits for screen time and stick to them.)

"WHAT IS THE CONTENT RATING? WHAT IS THE COMMITMENT LEVEL? WHAT IS THE CONNECTION TO OTHER PLAYERS?"
(Ask three questions about online games.)

When it comes to your child's engagement with technology, what do you hope is true for them 572 weeks from now?

_____

_____

_____

_____

_____

_____

_____

_____

_____

_____

_____

_____

_____

_____

_____

_____

_____

_____

_____

_____

What rules do you have for digital devices in your family? If you don't have any, what are two or three you might want to set for your second grader?

_____

_____

_____

_____

_____

_____

_____

_____

_____

_____

_____

_____

_____

_____

_____

_____

_____

_____

What are your own personal values and disciplines when it comes to leveraging technology? Are there ways you want to improve your own savvy, skill, or responsibility in this area?

_____

_____

_____

_____

_____

_____

_____

_____

_____

_____

_____

_____

_____

_____

_____

_____

_____

Authentic faith

—

TRUSTING JESUS
IN A WAY THAT
TRANSFORMS HOW
I LOVE GOD,
MYSELF,
AND THE REST
OF THE WORLD

THIS YEAR YOU WILL

PROVOKE DISCOVERY

SO YOUR CHILD WILL TRUST GOD'S CHARACTER AND EXPERIENCE GOD'S FAMILY.

Your second grader may be starting to enjoy reading. So, his is a great year to encourage skills that will help them enjoy reading the Bible. Make sure they have a full-text Bible in an easy-to-read translation, like the NIrV. Throughout your week, continue to talk about faith together.

SAY THINGS LIKE . . .

"CAN I PRAY ABOUT THAT WITH YOU?"

"YOU CAN TRUST GOD NO MATTER WHAT."

"YOU NEED TO MAKE THE WISE CHOICE."

"YOU SHOULD TREAT OTHERS THE WAY YOU WANT TO BE TREATED."

"WHEN I FIRST TRUSTED JESUS . . . "
(Share your own faith story.)

THE BIBLE HAS 66 BOOKS. THE BIG NUMBERS MARK THE CHAPTER, AND THE LITTLE NUMBERS MARK THE VERSE.
(Talk about the Bible.)

"OUR FAMILY SETS ASIDE 10% OF WHAT WE MAKE TO GIVE TO OUR CHURCH."
(Talk about how you manage finances as a response to God.)

"I LOVE THAT YOU NOTICED HOW THEY ARE FEELING. WHAT COULD WE DO TO HELP?"
(Encourage them to act on their impulses to help others.)

When it comes to your child's faith, what do you hope is true for them 572 weeks from now?

_____

_____

_____

_____

_____

_____

_____

_____

_____

_____

_____

_____

_____

_____

_____

_____

What adults are helping influence and develop your second grader's faith?

_____

_____

_____

_____

_____

_____

_____

_____

_____

_____

_____

_____

_____

_____

_____

_____

What routines or habits do you have in your own life that are stretching your faith?

_____

_____

_____

_____

_____

_____

_____

_____

_____

_____

_____

_____

_____

_____

_____

_____

_____

THE

OF YOUR

WEEK

—

WILL SHAPE

THE VALUES

IN YOUR

home.

NOW THAT YOU HAVE FILLED THIS BOOK WITH IDEAS AND GOALS, IT MAY SEEM AS IF YOU WILL NEVER HAVE TIME TO GET IT ALL DONE.

Actually, you have *572 weeks.*

And every week has potential.

The secret to making the most of this phase with your second grader is to take advantage of the time you already have. Create a rhythm to your weeks by leveraging these four times together.

Be a coach.
Instill purpose by starting the day with encouraging words.

Be a friend.
Interpret life during informal conversations as you travel.

Be a teacher.
Establish values with intentional conversations while you eat together.

Be a counselor.
Strengthen your relationship through heart conversations at the end of the day.

What are some of your favorite routines with your second grader?

_____

_____

_____

_____

_____

_____

_____

_____

_____

_____

_____

_____

_____

_____

_____

_____

Write down any other thoughts or questions about parenting your second grader.

_____

_____

_____

_____

_____

_____

_____

_____

_____

_____

_____

_____

_____

_____

_____

_____

_____

_____

_____

_____

_____

_____

_____

_____

_____

_____

_____

_____

_____

_____

_____

_____

_____

_____

_____

_____

_____

_____

_____

_____

_____

TO LOVE GOD

Provoke
discovery →

SO THEY WILL . . .
TRUST GOD'S CHARACTER
& EXPERIENCE GOD'S FAMILY

 WISDOM
(First day of school)

 FAITH
(Trust Jesus)

DO I HAVE YOUR ATTENTION?

DO I HAVE WHAT IT TAKES?

DO I HAVE FRIENDS?

K &
FIRST

SECOND
& THIRD

FOURTH
& FIFTH

ENGAGE their interests

EVERY KID → MADE IN THE IMAGE OF GOD

Incite
wonder   →   SO THEY WILL . . .
KNOW GOD'S LOVE
& MEET GOD'S FAMILY

BEGINNING
(Baby dedication)

AM I SAFE?	AM I ABLE?	AM I OKA
ZERO TO ONE	ONE & TWO	THREE & FOUR

EMBRACE *their physical needs*

YOU HAVE

APPROXIMATELY

572 WEEKS.

IT'S JUST

A PHASE

SO DON'T

MISS IT.

trust Jesus → TO HAVE A BETTER FUTURE

Fuel

passion   →   SO THEY WILL . . .
KEEP PURSUING AUTHENTIC FAITH
& DISCOVER A PERSONAL MISSION

 **FREEDOM**
(Driver's license)

 **GRADUATION**
(Moving on)

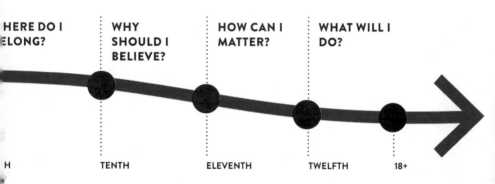

HERE DO I
ELONG?

**WHY
SHOULD I
BELIEVE?**

**HOW CAN I
MATTER?**

**WHAT WILL I
DO?**

H   TENTH   ELEVENTH   TWELFTH   18+

MOBILIZE *their potential*

WITH
ALL THEIR HEART SOUL  STRENGTH

Provoke
discovery $\longrightarrow$ SO THEY WILL . . .
OWN THEIR OWN FAITH
& VALUE A FAITH COMMUNITY

 **IDENTITY**
(Coming of age)

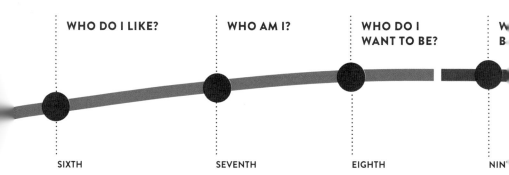

WHO DO I LIKE?   WHO AM I?   WHO DO I
WANT TO BE?   W
B

SIXTH   SEVENTH   EIGHTH   NIN

AFFIRM their personal journey

ABOUT THE AUTHORS

KRISTEN IVY @kristen_ivy

Kristen Ivy is executive director of the Phase Project. She and her husband, Matt, are in the preschool and elementary phases with three kids: Sawyer, Hensley, and Raleigh.

Kristen earned her Bachelors of Education from Baylor University in 2004 and received a Master of Divinity from Mercer University in 2009. She worked in the public school system as a high school biology and English teacher, where she learned firsthand the importance of influencing the next generation.

Kristen is also the President at Orange and has played an integral role in the development of the elementary, middle school, and high school curriculum and has shared her experiences at speaking events across the country. She is the co-author of *Playing for Keeps*, *Creating a Lead Small Culture*, *It's Just a Phase*, and *Don't Miss It*.

REGGIE JOINER @reggiejoiner

Reggie Joiner is founder and CEO of the reThink Group and co-founder of the Phase Project. He and his wife, Debbie, have reared four kids into adulthood. They now also have two grandchildren.

The reThink Group (also known as Orange) is a non-profit organization whose purpose is to influence those who influence the next generation. Orange provides resources and training for churches and organizations that create environments for parents, kids, and teenagers.

Before starting the reThink Group in 2006, Reggie was one of the founders of North Point Community Church. During his 11 years with Andy Stanley, Reggie was the executive director of family ministry, where he developed a new concept for relevant ministry to children, teenagers, and married adults. Reggie has authored and co-authored more than 10 books including: *Think Orange, Seven Practices of Effective Ministry, Parenting Beyond Your Capacity, Playing for Keeps, Lead Small, Creating a Lead Small Culture*, and his latest, *A New Kind of Leader* and *Don't Miss It.*

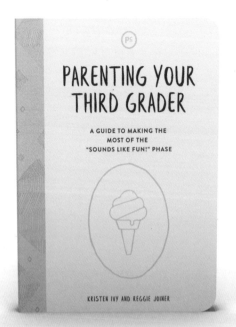

MAKE THE MOST OF EVERY PHASE IN YOUR CHILD'S LIFE

The guide in your hand is one of an eighteen-part series.

So, unless you've figured out a way to freeze time and keep your second grader from turning into a third grader, you might want to check out the next guide in this set.

Designed in partnership with Parent Cue, each guide will help you rediscover . . .

what's changing about your kid,
the 6 things your kid needs most,
and 4 conversations to have each year.

WANT TO GIFT A FRIEND WITH ALL 18 GUIDES
OR HAVE ALL THE GUIDES ON HAND FOR YOURSELF?

ORDER THE ENTIRE SERIES
OF PHASE GUIDES TODAY.